**Checkerboard
Library**

An Imprint of Abdo Publishing
abdopublishing.com

ABDOPUBLISHING.COM

Published by Abdo Publishing, a division of ABDO, PO Box 398166, Minneapolis, Minnesota 55439. Copyright © 2017 by Abdo Consulting Group, Inc. International copyrights reserved in all countries. No part of this book may be reproduced in any form without written permission from the publisher. Checkerboard Library™ is a trademark and logo of Abdo Publishing.

Printed in the United States of America, North Mankato, Minnesota
102016
012017

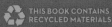

THIS BOOK CONTAINS
RECYCLED MATERIALS

Content Developer: Nancy Tuminelly
Design and Production: Mighty Media, Inc.
Series Editor: Rebecca Felix
Cover Photo: Getty Images
Interior Photos: AP Images, pp. 6, 9 (bottom), 11, 29; Getty Images, pp. 15, 17, 25; Library and Archives Canada, p. 8; Mighty Media, Inc., p. 23; National Archives and Records Administration/Wikimedia Commons, p. 19; Shutterstock Images, p. 23; Wikimedia Commons, pp. 5, 9 (top), 13, 21, 26

Publisher's Cataloging-in-Publication Data

Names: Mattern, Joanne, author.
Title: Technology during World War I / by Joanne Mattern.
Description: Minneapolis, MN : Abdo Publishing, 2017. | Series: Military
     technologies | Includes bibliographical references and index.
Identifiers: LCCN 2016944854 | ISBN 9781680784152 (lib. bdg.) |
     ISBN 9781680797688 (ebook)
Subjects: LCSH: United States--History--World War, 1914-1918--Technology--
     Juvenile literature. | Technology--United States--History--20th century--
     Juvenile literature.
Classification: DDC 940.3--dc23
LC record available at http://lccn.loc.gov/2016944854

THE WORLD AT WAR

In 1914, nations around the world engaged in a bloody battle. The fighting lasted four years. World War I was the first modern war between many different countries fighting on a global scale.

In the years before the war, European nations made several **alliances**. In 1882, Germany, Austria-Hungary, and Italy formed an alliance. In 1907, Great Britain, France, and Russia formed their own alliance.

These alliances required their members to support one another during conflict. They helped protect member nations. But they would also eventually pull many countries into war.

The spark that set off World War I happened in Eastern Europe. On June 28, 1914, a Serbian **assassinated** Archduke Franz Ferdinand, who was heir to the Austro-Hungarian throne. In return, Austria-Hungary attacked Serbia. Russia came to Serbia's aid.

The day after Ferdinand was assassinated, riots broke out in Serbia. Within one month, the first declaration of war was made.

Then Germany declared war on Russia in defense of its **alliance** with Austria-Hungary. Germany also declared war on France and Belgium. France and Great Britain declared war on Austria-Hungary. Britain also declared war on Germany. World War I had begun.

More than 4.7 million Americans served in World War I. Of these, more than 50,000 were soldiers who died in battle.

Across the Atlantic Ocean, many Americans did not want anything to do with the war. The United States remained **neutral**. Then in 1917, Germany broke a naval peace agreement it had with the United States. On April 6, the United States joined the **Allies**, declaring war on Germany. Germany led the **Central powers**.

During the war, troops fought long, bloody battles. Soldiers dug trenches and did much of their fighting from inside. They fired machine guns, threw **grenades**, and launched bombs.

Several armies waged chemical **warfare**, attacking their enemies with poison gases. And this war saw the introduction of two new **technologies**, the airplane and the submarine. These weapons would change how war was fought, both during World War I and in the future.

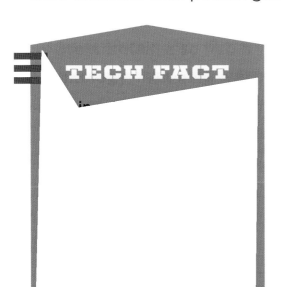

TECH FACT

JUNE 28, 1914
Austro-Hungarian Archduke Franz Ferdinand is **assassinated** in Serbia.

AUGUST 1914
Germany declares war on Russia, France, and Belgium. Great Britain declares war on Germany. France and Britain declare war on Austria-Hungary.

JULY 28, 1914
Austria-Hungary declares war on Serbia.

APRIL 22, 1915
Germany employs poison gas at the Second Battle of Ypres.

SEPTEMBER 1916

Great Britain introduces tanks at the Battle of the Somme.

DECEMBER 15, 1917

Russia signs an **armistice** with Germany and its **allies**.

APRIL 6, 1917

The United States declares war on Germany.

NOVEMBER 11, 1918

The armistice ends the fighting in Europe.

(2)

TRENCH WARFARE

Some of the bloodiest World War I battles were fought
by armies on the ground. And many of these conflicts
were actually fought *in* the ground! Armies on both sides
used trench **warfare**.

A basic trench was often more than 6 feet (1.8 m) deep
and 6 feet (1.8 m) wide. A ledge made of sandbags or
dirt lined the front of the trench. A raised wall ran along
the back.

Trenches were often dug at night so digging soldiers
were not exposed to enemy fire. Trenches were dug in a
zigzag pattern. This layout made it more difficult for the
enemy to fire into the trenches.

Rolls of **barbed wire** were laid across the ground in
front of the trenches. This was for protection. The wire
was layered, creating rows of tangled metal mesh.

At first, trenches were viewed as temporary shelters
during battles. However, as the war continued, it became

obvious to both sides that trench **warfare** would remain important. Some trenches held communication equipment and soldiers who operated it. Other trenches stored weapons and supplies.

Armies soon began building improved trenches. The sides were strengthened with wood to make them less likely to collapse from enemy fire. The Germans began using cement to **reinforce** underground trenches. Later, many **Allies** did the same.

INFANTRY AND ARTILLERY

During battle, bullets flew between trenches. The boom of **artillery** could be heard hundreds of miles away. The rifles and big guns used in World War I were key weapons for both the **Allies** and the **Central powers**.

The rifles soldiers used in World War I were improved **versions** of these earlier weapons. American soldiers used the Springfield M1903. Germans used Mauser rifles.

Both the M1903 and the Mauser rifle could hold five **rounds** at a time. As **technology** improved, new rifles were able to shoot more than one round at once.

Machine guns were a technology that brought a new level of death to the battlefield. They could shoot 400 to 600 bullets a minute. This also meant a large number of soldiers could be attacked and killed in only a minute.

Machine guns were mounted on supports that could be moved from place to place. To do this, each gun had a crew of three to six men. Some of the men fed bullets

into the gun using long cloth or metal strips. Other men poured water on the gun to keep it from overheating.

Large **artillery** was also an important weapon used during the war. This included cannons, howitzers, and mortars. These weapons were so large and heavy that they were often moved by railroad.

Artillery guns fired much larger shells than rifles and machine guns. The shells they fired were filled with explosives. These shells would **detonate** upon landing, killing or wounding anyone nearby.

POISON GASES

During World War I, armies used poison gases for the **first time.** Germans were first to use this type of weapon. These gases were delivered in **grenades** and **artillery** shells. They were also released from containers that were laid along trench lines.

The gases contained chemicals that burned the eyes, noses, and throats of those nearby. They made breathing difficult and burned the skin. Most poison gases could kill.

The leaders of many nations were critical of using poison gas in war. Many felt it was a cowardly weapon. In spite of these widespread beliefs, it did not take long for many nations to begin using them.

In 1917, armies on both sides began using mustard gas. This gas gave off a yellowish brown color.

Soldiers choked to death on mustard gas. They also suffered painful burns on their skin. Many went blind when the gas got into their eyes.

SECOND BATTLE OF YPRES

The Germans released about 6,000 containers of poisonous **chlorine** gas during the Second Battle of Ypres on April 22, 1915. Each container weighed 90 pounds (41 kg). The German soldiers marched toward French and Algerian trenches. They opened the containers and let the wind take over.

The wind carried the greenish-yellow cloud over the trenches, killing hundreds of soldiers and causing great panic. It was reported that many German soldiers died as well, from breathing in the gas as it drifted toward their enemies. Of the **Allies** that survived, many were taken prisoner as they ran out of the cloud. They were choking and unable to see from their blinded eyes.

POISON GAS ON THE BATTLEFIELD

Armies developed ways to protect themselves from poison gas. Soldiers were issued gas masks to protect them from harmful fumes. Each armies' gas masks were slightly different. But most worked similarly.

The US military designed its own type of mask. These masks completely covered the soldier's head and face. They had filters to help the soldier breathe in air without also breathing in the gas. These protective masks meant that poison gas attacks became much less deadly.

However, the thought of a gas attack still made soldiers nervous. So, this type of weapon had a powerful mental effect on armies in the field.

TANKS

Tough, armored **vehicles** known as landships became powerful new weapons in World War I. Later renamed tanks, these vehicles were large enough to carry several soldiers on or inside them. The tanks were covered in thick metal and fitted with guns.

Tanks were used for the first time in history during World War I. Britain introduced them at the Battle of the Somme in September 1916. They were developed to break the **stalemate** of trench **warfare**. Because soldiers could not leave their trenches without being killed by enemy fire, armies made little progress on the battlefield.

Tanks were a way to solve this problem. They could move over all types of land, including across trenches and over the **barbed wire** that protected them. The tanks' armor protected the soldiers inside from enemy fire.

Great Britain and France were the first nations to develop tanks. These tanks traveled up to

four miles per hour (6.4 kmh).
Instead of wheels, they moved on
two long metal belts. Tanks could
move over rough ground and obstacles without getting
stuck. Under the right conditions, one model of early
tanks could even climb a five-foot (1.5 m) wall!

When it first joined the war, the US military used
French-made Renault tanks. These tanks were light for
vehicles of this kind, weighing six tons (5.4 tonnes) each.
The United States later worked to develop its own tank,
the M1917. However, the war ended before it was finished
producing the M1917s. So, these tanks were never used in
combat.

THE WAR AT SEA

Explosive sea battles took place in every ocean around the world during the war. Advancements made to seacraft provided both sides with advantages. Navies employed many types of vessels on and below the water.

The Germans were famous for using undersea boats, or U-boats. They fired **torpedoes** from these submarines. At first, the Germans attacked mainly naval warships. Later, they began attacking nonmilitary ships.

Twice during the war, the Germans made agreements with the United States to stop attacking unarmed, **neutral** ships. But they later broke these promises. Soon after, in April 1917, the United States joined the fight, declaring war on Germany.

During the war, the US Navy sent cargo and transport ships, battleships, and destroyers across the ocean. Navy sailors used mines to attack the enemy. These bombs floated on or right under the ocean surface or were

planted on the sea floor. They
exploded on contact, damaging or
sinking passing ships or submarines.

The United States also developed
a type of warship to combat U-boats. These wooden
ships were called submarine chasers. They were 110 feet
(33.5 m) long and equipped with naval guns. Sailors sunk
many U-boats by dropping bombs called depth charges
from submarine chasers.

SUBMARINE CHASER

The submarine chaser used depth and naval gun charges to destroy enemy submarines. Depth charges were bombs made to **detonate** at a certain depth. Submarine chasers were also equipped with deck guns and machine guns. These boats traveled in groups of three called a hunting unit. Each mission was broken into three stages, called the hunt, the chase, and the attack.

THE HUNT

1. The hunting unit traveled to locations where enemy submarines were thought to be located. Each boat began searching, keeping several miles apart from one another.

2. Crew members listened for submarines by placing a hydrophone under the water. The hydrophone picked up the noise of submarine engines and **propellers**.

3. Once a submarine was detected, the boat that located it communicated with the hunting unit using radio devices, or signals. This boat became the lead chaser.

THE CHASE

4. The lead chaser would travel toward the submarine with its hunting unit following. When the lead chaser could confirm it

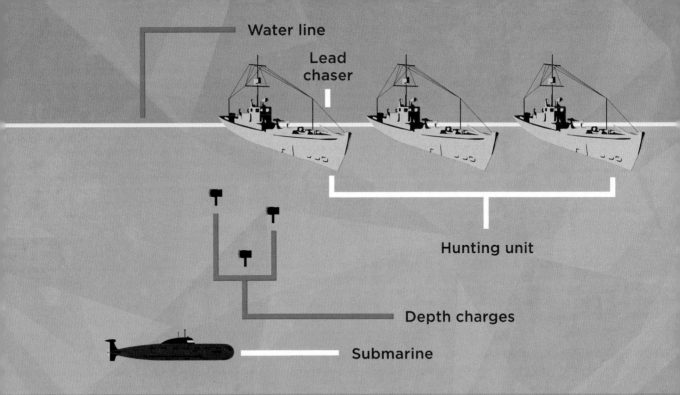

Water line

Lead chaser

Hunting unit

Depth charges

Submarine

was within 300 yards (274 m) of the enemy submarine, it was time to attack.

THE ATTACK

5. The lead chaser began dropping up to 18 depth charges into the water. The other boats in the hunting unit would also drop depth charges as they neared the submarine.

6. The hunting unit would travel away from the submarines, listening for the sounds of the bombs going off. Crews were prepared to attack with naval guns if a submarine rose.

AERIAL WARFARE

World War I was not won on land or sea alone. Motorized military airplanes took to the skies, joining the fight from the air. The airplane had been invented in the United States 11 years before the war began. During the war, aircraft were a key military weapon for both sides.

At first, planes were used for observation, not fighting. Some planes had enough room for a second person who could take photographs from the sky. These airmen also drew sketches and wrote down observations. These observations became very important. They allowed officers to see where enemy troops were located.

The world's first plane was invented in the United States. But the country's military was behind other nations in creating warplanes. US airmen

A US gunner fires at the enemy as the pilot navigates. The best pilots of World War I were called flying aces.

used French and British planes during much of World War I. One was the Sopwith Camel. This was a British-made plane that had two

The first Fokker Eindecker to successfully engage in air battle with a synchronization gear. The machine gun was mounted on top of the plane, above its nose and propeller.

mounted machine guns. It was considered difficult to fly, and so required an experienced pilot.

As the war continued, planes and **technology** improved. It did not take long before planes were an important part of the fighting.

Fighter planes battled in the sky. Small planes armed with machine guns fired at enemy planes in an attempt to shoot them down. And larger planes could carry and drop bombs on battlefields and cities.

In 1915, an important invention changed aerial combat. The German Fokker Eindecker airplane introduced the **synchronization** gear. This **technology** was attached to the nose of an airplane. It automatically fired machine guns that were mounted on the plane. The bullets would fly directly through the **propeller**. But the synchronization system was timed to hold fire when the blades passed in front of the gun's **muzzle**.

The synchronization gear made it easier for the pilot to fly and fire at the same time. With this system intact, the Fokker Eindecker became the deadliest weapon in the sky until the **Allies** could match its technology.

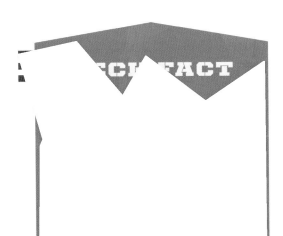

THE END OF THE WAR

By 1918, Germany was running out of supplies and soldiers. At the same time, large numbers of US soldiers had arrived in Europe. These armies won several major battles in 1918. It was clear that Germany would not win the war. An **armistice** was signed on November 11, 1918.

World War I remains one of the deadliest wars in history. By the end of the war, about 9 million soldiers had been killed and more than 20 million wounded. And an estimated 8 million nonmilitary citizens were killed by **warfare** as well.

The war introduced the widespread use of many **technologies**. Planes took to the skies in dogfights. Submarines destroyed both warships and merchant ships. Tanks rolled over trenches and through battlefields for the first time. And deadly poison gases were used to kill thousands of men silently. The use of these weapons and war **vehicles** gave each side an advantage in certain

November 11 became known worldwide as Armistice Day.

battles. And they would forever change the way future wars were fought on land, in the air, and at sea.

allies — people, groups, or nations united for some special purpose. The major allies in World War I were Great Britain, France, Italy, and the United States. A group of people or nations united for some special purpose is an alliance.

armistice — a pause in fighting brought about by an agreement between opponents.

artillery — large guns that can be used to shoot over a great distance.

assassinate — to murder a very important person, usually for political reasons.

barbed wire — wire that has sharp points and that is often used for fences.

Central powers — countries that fought together during World War I. Germany, Bulgaria, Austria-Hungary, and the Ottoman Empire made up the Central powers.

chlorine — a chemical that under normal conditions is a greenish-yellow gas and has a strong smell.

detonate — to set off an explosion.

grenade — a small bomb that is designed to be thrown by someone or shot from a rifle.

muzzle — the open front end of the barrel of a weapon.

neutral — not taking sides in a conflict.

propeller — a device that has a revolving central part with blades. The spinning blades move a vehicle, such as a boat or an airplane.

reinforce — to strengthen by adding materials or support.

round — a bullet, shell, or cartridge used for a single shot.

stalemate — a contest or battle in which neither side can gain an advantage or win.

synchronization — the act or result of causing things to happen at the same time and speed.

technology (tehk-NAH-luh-jee) — machinery and equipment developed for practical purposes using scientific principles and engineering.

torpedo — a submerged explosive.

vehicle — something used to carry or transport. Cars, trucks, airplanes, and boats are vehicles.

version — a different form or type of an original.

warfare — methods and weapons used to fight a war.